# Paul McGrane

# British People
# in Hot Weather

Indigo Dreams Publishing

First Edition: British People in Hot Weather
First published in Great Britain in 2021 by:
Indigo Dreams Publishing
24, Forest Houses
Cookworthy Moor
Halwill
Beaworthy
Devon
EX21 5UU

www.indigodreams.co.uk

ISBN 978-1-912876-61-7

British Library Cataloguing in Publication Data. A CIP record for this book can be obtained from the British Library.

Designed and typeset in Palatino Linotype by Indigo Dreams.
Cover design by Ronnie Goodyer at Indigo Dreams
Printed and bound in Great Britain by 4edge Ltd.

Papers used by Indigo Dreams are recyclable products made from wood grown in sustainable forests following the guidance of the Forest Stewardship Council.

For Sue Redpath –
because if it's not love then it's the bomb, the bomb, the bomb,
the bomb, the bomb, the bomb, the bomb that will bring us
together.

## Acknowledgements

'Valentine Tips for Boys' was published in *City Lights* (a tall-lighthouse anthology) and 'Search: Mark E Smith' was published in *Messing Up The Paintwork: The Wit and Wisdom of Mark E Smith* (Ebury Press/Penguin).

THANK YOU to past and present members of Forest Poets, Walthamstow, without whom these poems wouldn't exist.

'British People In Hot Weather' was the B side of 'Telephone Thing' by The Fall in January 1990. It reached the mighty height of number 58 on the UK singles chart.

**Also by Paul McGrane:**

Elastic Man (IDP, 2018)

# CONTENTS

# British People
# in Hot Weather

## Adolf Hitler European Tour

Not like it was a band I could believe
in or anything but I owned a pretty
cool t-shirt at the age of seventeen.
On the front was a full-colour cameo
of Adolf in profile, Nazi salute,
huge map of Europe in the background.
The reverse was like the tour dates for a group
but with, instead, the countries he'd invaded
listed chronologically, ending with
the bunker in Berlin. Britain was included
with cancelled in brackets. I loved that shirt.
It got me more attention than I'd
ever had before. My peak was at Glastonbury.
Two journos from the NME said wow
and took a photo. I bought the mag
for weeks but it never made it in.
It got a bit hectic, I'll admit,
when my father erupted as we sat
round the table, me in the shirt, fork
and knife ripping at the meat on his plate.
"Only stupid people have no sense of humour"
I squeaked at boiled potatoes in a bowl.
At the age of seventeen, I couldn't
look him in the eye when he was angry
which was, as I remember, all the time.

## Act

After I'd been chosen as the leading man,
that almost father of the only son of God,

mother found a robe that would cover up my clothes,
apart from pyjama legs poking out the bottom,

a towel for my head, fastened with a pin,
and a beard on a card stuck to a lolly stick.

She said Think of the Nativity without him.
How could young Mary ever manage on her own?

The real me could never talk to girls,
a boy who wouldn't stand out from the crowd,

but here was Joseph holding hands with Mary,
wise men and angels kneeling at his feet,

parents of the other children standing to applaud,
my mother in the middle of them all.

## leonard cohen's skin

father is pissing in the corner of my room
long-playing records stacked against the wall
some my own

most of them belonging to my brother
who left for good
and travels light

father leaves his bed
to find the house spun round
my room is where the toilet ought to be

father has been out
old cross inn and railway inn
rugby club and british legion

miners welfare golden grove
under father's flow
joni mitchell's eyes are acid yellow

leonard cohen's skin
wrinkled as he'll really be
forty years from now

## Settle

He told her he promised her he said
    the first drink was the last drink of the night
and so the trouble he was in
    was of his own making
He came home
    tumbling through the gate
He came home
    fumbling into bed
and as the sun rose
    fiery fingers scratching at his eyes
a nasty little terrorbird
    pecking at his skull
pain travelled on
    through the rest of his body
his lover having flown
    to the edge of the bed
As he slugged his way across
    miles and miles of mattress
    for some sympathy a hug
she scuffed his ragged hand
    from out of her way
as she might a sparrow
    in a garden on a breezy afternoon
coming in to land
    to settle
on the washing line
    a pillow
voluminous queen size
    lily-white sheets

## Your father's gone to stay with cousin Cyril for a while

After the screaming, my mother ran upstairs
leaving my father in the hallway by the door,
wood and metal clashing as she battled with the wardrobe,

throwing his clothes in a bin bag on the bed.
If there'd ever been a day when they had love for one another,
by the time I came around that day had gone.

Bad husband, he was very rarely in,
spending all his time in the pub or the garden
sweet-talking seedlings into flower

but when they'd share a room
ice hung from the ceiling
and every cough or sigh could spark an argument.

TV turned up loud would obliterate the noise.
A cat would chase a mouse with a machete,
the mouse would take revenge with a pitchfork to the neck.

I'd be out of there as soon as I was old enough to leave.
The bin bag was left out on the street.
We were a one-parent family for a week.

## Spreading the word

As regular as Santa Claus, she'd call
around at Christmas, the next-door neighbour
and my Sunday school teacher, Mrs Williams.
My mother sent me searching for the matching
cup and saucer, television off
for the only time that year. Hello
Mrs Williams, how nice of you to call.
Mince pie. Three or four sugars in her tea.

She was a bit of a bragger, Mrs
Williams, and seemed quite la dee da, though
she lived in a council house like everybody
else. She'd tell us how her daughter's kids, Camella
and Estella, were flying high at school,
swimming for the county, writing, in French
and in verse, to pen pals in Paris.

She was big on religion, Mrs Williams,
I'd heard her say that people die and somehow
rise again but, at least on her visits,
she would not mention God. Instead, after
one last cup of tea, a disappointing
present in the form of a book where every
year the storyline was more or less the same –
inner city boys and girls in trouble
with the law and a man in plastic collar
who'd come to the rescue. I'd read them once
and throw them all away.

What if
it wasn't just me? What if all the other kids
were given books to read where Christians
always win? As a Sunday school teacher,
she must have had a large supply to hoik
from door-to-door and around the estate,
bent by the weight of a satchel on her back,
supermarket carry bags dragging through
the snow. Wrapping paper, greeting cards,
Sellotape and books. So many children
to see, she might have had to knock on doors
as early as November. *Bore da,*
*Mrs Williams, sut dych chi*? Gallons of tea.
Bladder the size of a Christmas stocking.

*Bore da... sut dych chi?:* Good morning... how are you?

## Kissing

We'd watch them on TV,
the middle classes,
on comedies and dramas or
anything with wine, the wearing
of suits.
For no apparent reason
they'd be kissing all the time,
hellos and goodbyes,
lunches and dinners,
parents kissing children,
the children kissing back,
as though they hadn't met
in donkey's years
when mainly it was less
than half an hour.
They'd kiss more than they'd
speak to one another.
Not us.
Xmas, birthdays and my
first day at school,
my cheek would stay untouched.
The only time I tried
was when I launched myself
to college.
A peck.
A reminder, should she need,
that I'd be absent for a bit.
Nothing was said
but her quick look
at my father
meant
see how he's changed.

## The first and only dinner with my uncle

You heard I served in Burma just after the war?
A gorgeous little thing she was.
So you're not the only person with a taste for the exotic.
Don't tell your auntie, by the way.
That was all over long before we met,
before we married.

Second cousin Cyril said he saw you.
It's not for me to say
but he must have been wondering
what can he be thinking of
holding hands with her?
He phoned your father and your father phoned me.

Be careful while you're here.
We're small town people
and everyoneknowseveryone.
It's your dad who'll take the blame.
Do what you like when you're back in the city.
But you're right when you say it's none of my business.

## Visiting the Old Folks

Do we have to go?
It's only for the weekend.
Grit your teeth and sparkle.

Up with the foxes.
Driving through the London rain.
Last decent music.

Croeso i Gymru.
You're welcome to Port Talbot.
Stinks in the nostrils.

Don't know anyone.
Chocker with kids and grannies.
Where's the Co-Op gone?

Hasn't he got fat.
Which road did you take this time?
Don't you sound English.

Round the square table.
Carrots boiled for half an hour.
Telly on full blast.

The photo album.
Trapped in front of Songs of Praise.
Feel like I'm six.

Unable to fart.
Can't stretch out on the sofa.
Can't find a corkscrew.

We'd love to stay but...
Got to work Monday.
Don't be a stranger.

Thank God it's over.
Brownie points for a few months.
It wasn't so bad.

## Names, words, etcetera

Everyone smiled, if I remember right,
and the room would fill with nudges and winks
as we tried to unravel who he meant
when a friend was called You know, whatsisname
or a word used a zillion times before
would become You know, whatchamacallit
or a sentence would start but seldom end
without a helping hand to guide him home

but when his key failed to open the door
of a house he was long forgotten in
and they said he had to count the week backwards
or when he asked me in the hospital
if he'd loved, or had ever been loved,
nobody smiled, as far as I recall.

## Social Distancing

I haven't talked to my dad for a while.
There's an underlying reason –
he's been dead for twenty years.
Even back then, when he'd life
in the lungs and skin on the bone,
he'd see but look straight through me.
To him I was something that
my mother should take care of
like cooking and cleaning and the washing up.
In rare times, the two of us alone,
I'd hear the roar of the wind
through the whiskers of a mouse
somewhere at the far end of the world.

## Need

He's tapping at the door,
lets the light in gently with a push.
Do you need? he says to the darkness.
Every night her crying haunts the house,
wakes him when he ought to be asleep.
Hup we get. He helps her out of sheets
heavier than her, shouldering
her body to the potty in the corner.
There we go Mam, pulling up
her nightie, trying not to look.
Shout when you're ready, he says,
slipping into light again and waiting.

## Thrift

*for my mum, born by the sea*

pompom head
of pinksoft
bloom
homesick
for the marriages
of bees
on sand
and coastal cliff
tiny flower
slender stem
if only i
had known you
there
in the worry
of my garden
nettlestung
and strangled
wrongwardly facing
from the sun

# Migrant Mother

*after a photograph by Dorothea Lange*

A quick calculation.
My mother was twelve when this photo was taken.
This woman looks three times that age
at least.
My mother had better clothes, less kids to cling to,
and she knew where her next meal was coming from.
We would certainly all have had a wash,
and we would have all been fighting,
screaming in colour,
not still,
exhausted,
like these.

The year is different and so is the continent
but I've seen the eyes of this woman before,
vivid with despair,
wondering where her life has gone,
desperate for the burden to go away,
but not desperate enough to say it out loud,
not that anyone would hear her if she did.

Her eyes are so powerful
you could do anything with the rest of the photograph:
lose the kids and give her a boob job,
introduce make-up,
put her next to a swimming pool in a bikini
with champagne in her hand,
call it Lottery Winner Celebrates,
intend it to be happiness portrayed,
put a smile on her face
but keep the eyes in and the message is
Go. Leave me. Save yourself.

I'd like to think
that if I saw a fellow human being
in distress
I'd instinctively want to give them a hug,
tell them it will all be OK,
or at least want to,
but those eyes aren't looking for something
as pointless
as sympathy or love.
They say Leave me alone or I'll drag you down with me.
And I'd go in a shot without even a thank you.

I have a theory,
formed in the last few minutes,
that these eyes could be taken out of the photo altogether
and transferred onto a living person
you don't associate with misery.
David Dickenson, perhaps.
Dawn French.
Tony Blair.
*Lionel* Blair.
You.
And yes, even me.
At some points in our lives
we all look like this
but only people who care for us will see
or people
like Dorothea
who specialise in these off-camera moments
on camera.

To test the theory,
I look in the mirror
to capture that look.
I can't.
None of us can.

The human spirit stops us from exposing it
to the public
or even to ourselves.
Especially ourselves.
It can't allow us
to look defeated,
forces us to show
that we carry on regardless,
that shit happens
but we get on with it.

And I bet
once she realised the photo had been taken
or when one of the kids demanded attention
her eyes gleamed she was OK.
Not starving.
Not failing to cope.
Not lost and lonely.
OK.

After thinking about this
for too long,
I went out of my way
to say hello
to a stranger
I'd otherwise have walked past
and ignored.
I said Morning, lovely day
in my best Welsh accent
so I could pretend I was new to London
and unfamiliar with the rules.
He grunted back
like I was about to mug him,
or insane.

I thought Miserable git
and walked on,
slightly embarrassed by my actions,
vowing not to do this again,
but,
for the briefest of moments,
I caught a glimpse of his eyes.
They sparkled.

## dreamfather

on ammanford high street
hand in hand with dad
begging daddy please
show me how to fly
he lifts me then
beyond the road
the cars
and yes
the tallest trees
height I could not reach
for on my own
and while the world
is dark and ready
for a fight
sky is safe
and always blue
dad is here
dad is watching out

my dreamfather
more loving version
of the man I knew
sadly your deeds
are here undone
but let this lie
of a relationship
mad comparison
keep coming at me nights
now you have gone

## Danny the Dap

When I think of school I think of
the assembly hall that doubled as
a gym on Wednesday afternoons
in a time when smacking children
was a part of the curriculum. He
stuck me in the team who struggled
on the vaulting horse, the climbing
frame and trampoline. The more
I'd fail, the more he'd shout my name
and his saying of it meant I kept on
failing. Muck Crane! without the
'silent sea' or G, as though he thought
to punish me with mispronunciation,
to emphasise the difference, to separate
me out, from Williamses and Thomases,
Joneses, Hughes and Evanses, the
proper Welsh. I can see myself loudly,
my body slowing down to almost next
to nothing, as if to say I'd never need
the skills he failed to teach, and how
could I be failing if I wasn't really
trying to succeed? With other boys
laughing, he sent me to the changing
room, long before the bell, to sob among
the lockers on my own, his nickname
a warning of what was coming next.

*Dap: (Wales) plimsoll / training shoe*

## My dearest Alfredo

I trust that my letter has found you.
I have written many times with no reply.

Since the death of Violetta, God rest
her soul, you have been so long away

anyone might say she was your sweetheart.
If so, I pray you were loved more than I, brother.

My opulent husband is
of father's choosing

and tomorrow marks another year,
a most unhappy marriage.

We hardly talk, we touch
as though by accident.

Already I have lost one
child but another is due.

If the baby is a boy I will name
him after you should father allow.

He speaks of you quite often. I hope you
can forgive him, whatever he has done.

Dear heart, perhaps I'll see you soon,
at least on the day of the christening?

There will be dancing and
singing and father will pay.

Please say you will come. Lord
knows we all deserve some happiness.

Ever your beloved sister.

*In Verdi's opera, La Traviata, the sister is referred to but not named.
Her father brings the relationship between Alfredo and Violetta ('the
fallen woman') to an end so that his daughter's chance of a respectable
marriage is not impacted by family scandal.*

## Fluff

From a window at my house I could look across
the field to a bus stop with a shelter and a bench.
I once saw Andrew Davies there, his hand
down the skirt of a girl I don't know.
He died in a car he tried the handle of.
His father proved that hair can be white overnight.
The kind of lad my parents had to tell me   Stay Away.

He'd always ride a swing beyond the furthest reach.
He broke a soldier doll, tore its voice out
when he pulled the string too hard.
He hurled bricks at a building
where they used to slaughter pigs.
You could hear the smash of glass
from both ends of the valley.

I ended us as friends when he said to Gary Evans
I could beat him in a fight
just so he could watch me getting beat up in a fight.
He was in that car, Gary Evans.
I've looked him up on Facebook.
Ex-army, kids, a Doberman Pinscher
that looks nothing like her name.

## Built to last

These'll do, he said.
*Prodotto a Venezia.*
Mouth-blown by Italians on the island of Murano.
From liquid sand to works of art.
So delicate of stem
and if I tap one with my nail
speeches will be given at a wedding,
choirs will be practising their scales.

No, she said, you're wrong.
The glasses we'll be buying will be far from Fancy Dan.
They'll pay for their keep in water and wine
and when they land on hardened floors,
when they drop from slippy hands,
they'll never crack.

Thirty years later he remembers what she said.
You're right, he says, his glass raised to the air.
Their glasses clink together like a yes.

## Ha Ha you say

Pigeons bomb the benches
round the fountain,
Leicester Square.
My arm has been hit
by a splash of hot porridge
    HelluvaSurprise.
No harm done. No-one is to blame.
They are, after all, only animals
and the splash has only landed
on a naked limb.
Sandals, shorts and t-shirt all OK.
This Pret A Manger serviette
will clean the poop away.
*Ha Ha* you say
but the joke is on you:
slime green mayonnaise
    yuck
in your black Americano
and your beautiful hair.

## Valentine Tips for Boys

Fellas, I wore my heart covered boxer shorts, scissor
tight under my trousers. The morning started with flowers
from Sainsbury's (a single rose is too traditional),
poetry in my handwriting. An earlier little ditty
had been read at The Orient. It said: 'Love you until
the O's win the Premiership'. I'd done the dinner with
careful co-ordination (we're not talking pizza!),
the hot lipped confetti dotting the table from
me to her and round again. The candles burned for her,
the champers popped and fizzed. Starters? Prosciutto
and smoked salmon salad, rocket, cress, shredded radicchio.
Then succulent sirloin, pepper pink in the middle,
crush (on you) potatoes, sexy shallots, garlic,
our mouths on fire with the Shiraz berry flavours.
And then I made my mistake. During the mood music,
the perfect formula to make her shoulders swing –
opera (Mozart, La Trav, a bit of Puccini);
Ella and her fellas (*into each life a little*
*rain must fall)*; Billie (*Tears in my dreams, rocks in my*
*heart)*; the two of us trying to Sing-a-longa-Nina,
(Nina Simone, not Nana Mouskouri), it was such a bloody
irony that in my sudden, drunken need for
noise, I surprised her with *Closer* by the boys from
Joy Division, dividing us, spoiling her evening
(even Amaretto could no longer sweeten her).
I know, now, it was a no-no (should've known on
the night), even though it would've been ok the
night before, the night after. So, when we should have ended
up in bed, together, I was left alone, washed
up with the dirty plates and coffee cups, drinking

the dregs from the bottle. On the shuffle CD
Ian Curtis sang to me: *'and we're changing our ways,*
*taking different roads. Then love, love will*
*tear us apart again'.* Ignoring his message,
I fled the filthy dishes and scrambled up, bowed,
to her snoring softly sound.

## Nature

In a passenger seat on Remembrance Sunday,
a blue November morning calls for moments of reflection.
Our minds closed by doors all week,
hands held for warmth are pulled to the ancient breeds.

We know all about them but still read the signs.
Five ladies. Rosie and Violet, the Longhorns;
Felicia and Felicity, the Belted Middles;
Kelly the solitary Dexter.

Varieties of wild flowers, grass munched contentedly,
daily repetition and all girls together.
I wonder out loud why animals stay so super-close
when they could go wherever,

and you repeat a fact you heard on TV
something about security, a twitch alerting the others.
You come out with more as a squirrel crosses over:
They scratch trees as a distraction from stress,

endanger the tree in the process.
They cheat on their mate…
remember where they're buried…
eat them when they're not looking.

A wheeze of white feathers points the way forward.
One breaks rank but is quickly tucked in.
A dogless man scares wings off the riverbed.
We find no noses to pat at the riding school.

It must be Nature's day off, I say,
as we wait for our number to be called at the caff.
The hot soup keeps out the noise from screaming babies.
Somewhere on another table we hear:

The blacks deflower virgins for the removal of AIDS.
The stress on blacks has wound me up –
We all stick our cocks into anything,
I shout –

especially virgins, and we don't give a fuck.
As my ignorance fights ignorance, I laugh.
Back at the car, you check your Walk-O-Meter,
miffed, as you hoped we'd come further.

**Ark**

The sky has been dark for more than a year
but we thought we'd be okay, we'd still have

each other and the rest of our lives,
the light would unfurl sooner or later.

Today is the end for us, honey.
Above and around us all we can hear,

all we can see, is sludgy rain. When we
run with the animals down to the shore,

frenzy of excrement, feathers and fur,
we'll be buried in sand or end as

bloated bodies rotting in the sea, boats
we fail to scramble on drifting out of sight,

the tallest of the creatures on the upper decks
waving at us, baby, with their necks.

## Date

We meet not as lovers
but as strangers who once knew each other well

We haven't been together since I broke
the neck of Christmas and brought us to an end

I bend to kiss your cheek but you pull away
You're Fine and I'm Yeah, fine

We thank each other very much for asking
I order wine from Poo-glee-a, crud-ites

when it should be croo-da-tay,
My mispronunciation is reflected in your scowl

In case of running out of stuff to say
I shuffle photographs, slide

them along to your end of the table
There's a few of me and her

a blur on the dancefloor
and the beach

You leave with your starter
in a paper serviette

the cork stays in the bottle
your wine glass is an empty glass of wine

That café's been and gone
I miss the spicy sausages and penne

and ooo that frozen chocolate cake
with raisins soaked in brandy

## Press Gang

Brigstock Weaver
of The Mary and Martha
was caught at St Kitts
and forced to loot ships
from there to Newfoundland.
Chased by The Navy,
he made it to England
and was nabbed by a captain
whose ship he had raided.
Sentenced to hang, he was let
off the hook by proving that
pirates had made him take part.

Jaden Moodie's mum
found a knife in his room.
She sent him to London
to stay with his gran
where all that he owned
he owed to the gang –
love and respect,
money from dealing
and low-level crime.
He was free of the gang
when dead in the street
at the age of fourteen.

**going viral**

to save the world from corona
he sings the red flag while washing his hands
but the only line he knows is where the flag is flying high
so he'll stick to happy birthday from now on
he uses a hand to turn off the tap
there's a queue for the dryer so he wipes
his soaking hands on the back of his trousers
and the front of his shirt job done
door knob and stair rail on the way to the bar
where friends have arrived
handshakes fist bumps hi fives and hugs
with a borrowed biro which he chews
he takes down what they want
four pints of lager g & t with ice
glass of prosecco diet coke
grabbing handfuls of peanuts from a bowl at the bar
he cleans his salty fingers with a hanky
he's been sneezing in all week
his throat hurts and he coughs
it could be the nuts but he googles the symptoms
his finger leaving smudges on the surface of the screen

## Performance

Every hour, on the hour,
I thought it had said
but at five minutes past
nothing has happened.
The shops are shut.
The market stallholders have gone.
Just this man
outside the fishmonger,
Walthamstow High Street.
He's mopping up,
slopping out,
getting ready,
I assume,
for the imminent performance
or I may
have got the venue wrong,
the day.

Lucky there's a programme I can check:

*Venue 37. Art Night at the N & A Fish Shop*
*(fresh fish from all over the world).*
*Watch as Mr Brusherman,*
*in overalls and wellingtons,*
*hoses down his counter,*
*washing water out the door*
*until it dissipates.*
*A collaborative portrait of the ritual of work.*
*A hymn to the market after dark.*
*The everyday as seldom seen before.*
*A paean to industry.*
*No booking necessary. Free.*

The morning after, everything is Art.
I stand to applaud
an elderly gentleman
crossing at the lights,
put my hands together
for the honeysuckle
bobbing in the rain
and when a robin wins a battle
with a worm –
Bravo Mr Robin! Encore! Encore!

## Eau de

I'd rather be
at work
with the recently exhumed
than the man
with malodorous perfume.
You have to stop
breathing
for a while
when he walks
in the room.
Flies,
who breathe
in a different way,
are flip-flopped
on their backs,
waggle-legs
pointing
up to Heaven.
If I knew
how to burgle,
I would find out
where he lives,
flushing the aroma
down the loo.
Goodbye fish,
currently alive,
soon to be afloat
on the surface
of the sea!

## Unit 8 / Series 53 has died
## (and, oh, the difference to me)

He talked too much, or so they claimed,
the reason why they let him go.
I don't think so.
We'd chat each day, it's true.
The usual subjects. Weather, sport,
the pros and cons of civil rights for robots.
But only for a while.
In a meeting, however, they agreed
I'd be far more productive if he left.
I was let off with a warning.
His replacement has been put on Quiet Mode,
forbidden to speak
when side-by-side with humans.
I miss the original. His smile.
The soft radio-interference in his voice
as he said his last goodbyes.
He told me he looked forward
to this unexpected break,
a chance to get some fat on his bones.
I read in the old days we'd be given
time for something called a Funeral.
I tell my new co-worker but she's programmed not to listen.
Tomorrow, they'll be testing me for Feelings.
If they find some I'll be in for further trouble.

## Dying Words of Patrick Moore

The Martians
live
in houses
just like yours

with chimney
roof
four windows
and a door

Instead
of humans
Martians
live inside

I may
have said
they don't exist
I lied

**Elsie**

On August sixteenth each year
she wears an Elvis wig in the shower

For her eightieth
she had an Elvis Presley tattoo on her bum

She has Elvis mugs coasters slippers tea towels
wallpaper and pens

She has hamsters called Memphis and Mississippi
and a cat called King

Elsie talks about Elvis Presley night and day
She's had five husbands

She divorced the first
when he shaved off his sideburns and grew a moustache

If she'd had a child
she would have called it Elvis or Lisa Marie

Elvis was so young when she was in her twenties
Now everyone is

Elsie likes to dance but she can't gyrate her hips
now that they're plastic

Elsie doesn't talk to Ethel
because Ethel prefers Cliff Richard

The doctor doesn't like it
when she calls this place the heartbreak hotel

She's taken uppers and downers just like Elvis
but she's still alive

Elsie wants to die sitting on the toilet
burger in her mouth

She's not religious
If there is a god she hopes he looks like Elvis

Elsie has never caught a rabbit
but she is a good friend of mine

## Peacock

From the gardens of Castelo San Jorge
come the screams of a damsel in distress
as loud as a car alarm at midnight
or laughter from a party held next door.
It must be a maiden being murdered
by a beast who is virtually human,
letters spelling R-E-V-E-N-G-E
in blood on four of his fists.
All this I can hear from the nearest hotel
through a window as thin as a feather
in the pillow I hide my head under.
I will rescue you in the morning, Princess.
It won't take me long to throw on my armour.
For now, please, I beg you, let me rest.

## Search: Mark E Smith

Remarkably there are a lot of them,
even though the middle E
was meant to mark him out from all the other Smiths.
According to socials he's either
Recruitment Manager at a well-known online retailer
(you'll know the one),
a North of England University Vice-Chancellor,
Actor slash Violinist slash Singer,
Water Resources Lecturer –
tweets are his own –
Mobility Superstar,
author, speaker,
everything mobility his passion,
sounds organiser
from Denver, Colorado,
election boycott advocate – don't vote! –
learns Chinese Kung Fu under Siu Barry Gray,
Newark, New Jersey,
Christian music lover,
reluctant teacher,
married to Queen Laura,
the most wonderful woman ever,
one year older than he was last year,
or the real Mark, uncommon,
gone, and what will we all do now?

Indigo Dreams Publishing Ltd
24, Forest Houses
Cookworthy Moor
Halwill
Beaworthy
Devon
EX21 5UU
www.indigodreams.co.uk